# Just between You and Me

A MOTHER - DAUGHTER JOURNAL

Lively Lines Publishing

# How to use this Journal?

**Set a Regular Schedule:**
Decide how often you'll exchange the journal. It could be weekly, or monthly. Consistency helps build a habit and makes each entry something to look forward to.

**Use the Prompts:**
Throughout the journal, you'll find various prompts and activities. These are starting points meant to inspire deeper conversations and reflections. Don't feel restricted by these prompts; feel free to express whatever is on your mind or heart.

**Be Honest and Open**:
The strength of this journal lies in honesty and openness. Share your true thoughts and feelings. This is a safe space for both of you to express yourselves without judgment.

**Keep it Private:**
Agree to keep the contents of the journal between the two of you, unless otherwise discussed. Respect for each other's privacy will foster trust and openness.

**Decorate and Personalize**: Make this journal uniquely yours. Add photos, drawings, stickers, or anything else that helps illustrate your entries and makes the journal more engaging and personal.

# Table of contents


| | |
|---|---|
| Beginning Informations | 5 |
| Family Memories | 13 |
| Traditions and Celebrations | 25 |
| School zone | 37 |
| Friendship and Relationships | 43 |
| Women's Wisdom | 61 |
| Dreams and Desires | 71 |
| Gratitude and Appreciations | 83 |
| Adventures and Experiences | 89 |
| Hopes for the Future | 101 |
| Notes | 109 |

# This journal belongs to:

Name:

Name:

Affectionately called:

Affectionately called:

We start this journey with:

# What are we like?

| Mom<br>Daughter writes | Daughter<br>Mom writes |
| --- | --- |
| 1. ........................................ | 1. ........................................ |
| 2. ........................................ | 2. ........................................ |
| 3. ........................................ | 3. ........................................ |
| 4. ........................................ | 4. ........................................ |
| 5. ........................................ | 5. ........................................ |

# I love you for...

| Daughter writes | Mom writes |
| --- | --- |
| 1. ........................................ | 1. ........................................ |
| 2. ........................................ | 2. ........................................ |
| 3. ........................................ | 3. ........................................ |
| 4. ........................................ | 4. ........................................ |
| 5. ........................................ | 5. ........................................ |

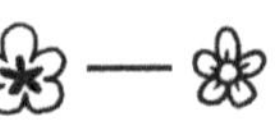

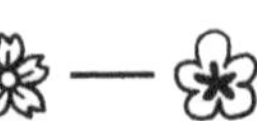

# Understanding Each Other

## Our relationship

| Mom | Daughter |
|---|---|
| 1. ........................................ | 1. ........................................ |
| 2. ........................................ | 2. ........................................ |
| 3. ........................................ | 3. ........................................ |
| 4. ........................................ | 4. ........................................ |
| 5. ........................................ | 5. ........................................ |

## Our Values

| Mom | Daughter |
|---|---|
| 1. ........................................ | 1. ........................................ |
| 2. ........................................ | 2. ........................................ |
| 3. ........................................ | 3. ........................................ |
| 4. ........................................ | 4. ........................................ |
| 5. ........................................ | 5. ........................................ |

# Beginning Questions

Is there anything specific you hope to learn about me/you through this journal?

How do you think this journal might change or enhance our relationship?

What are your favorite ways to express yourself creatively?

MOM

# Beginning Questions

Is there anything specific you hope to learn about me/you through this journal?

How do you think this journal might change or enhance our relationship?

What are your favorite ways to express yourself creatively?

# Beginning Questions

How often do you think we should write in this journal, and why?

How do you feel about sharing and discussing our entries with each other?

If you could describe your hopes for this journal in three words, what would they be?

MOM

# Beginning Questions

How often do you think we should write in this journal, and why?

How do you feel about sharing and discussing our entries with each other?

If you could describe your hopes for this journal in three words, what would they be?

# The Joy in Our Lives

## What Makes Us Happy

| Mom | Daughter |
| --- | --- |
| 1. ........................................ | 1. ........................................ |
| 2. ........................................ | 2. ........................................ |
| 3. ........................................ | 3. ........................................ |
| 4. ........................................ | 4. ........................................ |
| 5. ........................................ | 5. ........................................ |

## Places We Dream of Visiting

| Mom | Daughter |
| --- | --- |
| 1. ........................................ | 1. ........................................ |
| 2. ........................................ | 2. ........................................ |
| 3. ........................................ | 3. ........................................ |
| 4. ........................................ | 4. ........................................ |
| 5. ........................................ | 5. ........................................ |

# Family Memories

# Family Memories

What is your favorite memory of us together?

What do you think is the key to a happy family life?

What do you admire most about our family?

# Family Memories

What is your favorite memory of us together?

What do you think is the key to a happy family life?

What do you admire most about our family?

# Family Memories

Is there something you've always wanted to ask me but haven't?

Is there a song or movie that always reminds you of our family? Why?

# Family Memories

Is there something you've always wanted to ask me but haven't?

Is there a song or movie that always reminds you of our family? Why?

# Family Memories

Can you think of a moment when you felt extremely proud to be a part of our family?

What's a habit or trait that you've picked up from our family?

How do you hope our family will be remembered in the future?

# Family Memories

Can you think of a moment when you felt extremely proud to be a part of our family?

What's a habit or trait that you've picked up from our family?

How do you hope our family will be remembered in the future?

Memory Map

Create a 'Memory Map' of your trips, excursions or other important moments together.

# Time capsule

Create a 'Time Capsule' in your journal. Write down current interests, favourite things, friends, as well as your thoughts and hopes for the future on a piece of paper. Put the letter in an envelope and paste it there. Decide when you will open it again - maybe in a year, two years or more....

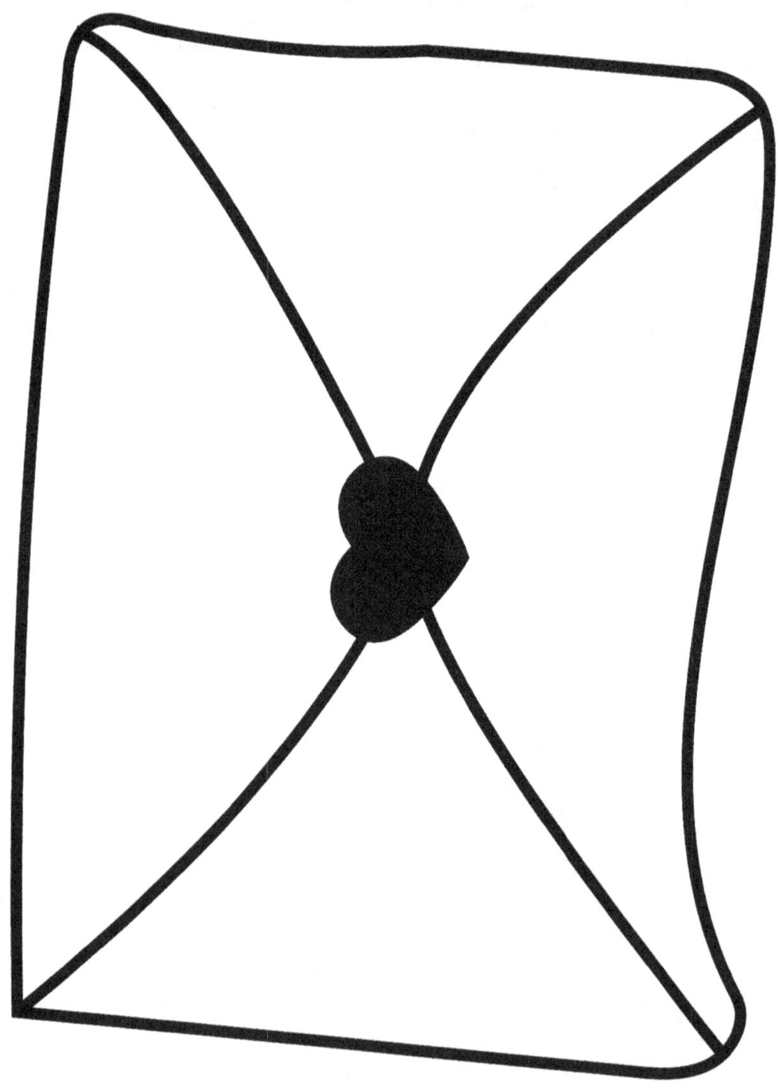

# Traditions and Celebrations

# Family Traditions

Is there a tradition that you hold dear to your heart? Why is it meaningful to you?

Have you ever wanted to start a new tradition? What would it be and why?

What's the most important lesson you've learned from our family's traditions and celebrations?

MOM

# Family Traditions

Is there a tradition that you hold dear to your heart? Why is it meaningful to you?

Have you ever wanted to start a new tradition? What would it be and why?

What's the most important lesson you've learned from our family's traditions and celebrations?

# Celebration Wheel

This wheel is divided into segments, each designed for a different family celebration or tradition. Within each segment, there's space for writing about the tradition, and sharing why it's meaningful.

# Celebration Planner

Plan a future celebration together. It could be a birthday, holiday, or a new tradition you want to start. Outline the activities, food, and any special rituals you want to include.

| JANUARY | FEBRUARY | MARCH |
|---|---|---|
| | | |

| APRIL | MAY | JUNE |
|---|---|---|
| | | |

| JULY | AUGUST | SEPTEMBER |
|---|---|---|
| | | |

| OCTOBER | NOVEMBER | DECEMBER |
|---|---|---|
| | | |

# Our family recipes

**NAME OF DISH**

DIFFICULTY ○○○○○

PREP TIME

COOK TIME

**INGREDIENTS**

**DIRECTIONS**

notes

# Our family recipes

**NAME OF DISH**

DIFFICULTY ○○○○○

PREP TIME

COOK TIME

**DIRECTIONS**

**INGREDIENTS**

notes

# Our family recipes

**NAME OF DISH**

DIFFICULTY ○○○○○

PREP TIME

COOK TIME

**INGREDIENTS**

**DIRECTIONS**

notes

# Our family recipes

NAME OF DISH

DIFFICULTY ○○○○○

PREP TIME

COOK TIME

**DIRECTIONS**

**INGREDIENTS**

notes

# Our family recipes

**NAME OF DISH**

DIFFICULTY ○○○○○

PREP TIME

COOK TIME

**INGREDIENTS**

**DIRECTIONS**

notes

# Our family recipes

**NAME OF DISH**

DIFFICULTY ○○○○○

PREP TIME

COOK TIME

**DIRECTIONS**

**INGREDIENTS**

notes

# Our family recipes

NAME OF DISH

DIFFICULTY ○○○○○

PREP TIME

COOK TIME

INGREDIENTS

DIRECTIONS

notes

# Our family recipes

**NAME OF DISH**

DIFFICULTY ○○○○○

PREP TIME

COOK TIME

**DIRECTIONS**

**INGREDIENTS**

notes

# Our family recipes

NAME OF DISH

DIFFICULTY ○○○○○

PREP TIME

COOK TIME

INGREDIENTS

DIRECTIONS

notes

# Our family recipes

**NAME OF DISH**

DIFFICULTY

PREP TIME

COOK TIME

**DIRECTIONS**

**INGREDIENTS**

notes

# Our family recipes

**NAME OF DISH**

DIFFICULTY ○○○○○ | PREP TIME | COOK TIME

**INGREDIENTS**

**DIRECTIONS**

notes

# School zone

# First day at School

Share memories of your first day at school. Try to remember how you felt when you entered the classroom, who you met, what you saw, and how the day ended. Mention any advice or reassurance your parents gave you that day.

# First day at School

# School zone

What was your favorite subject at school and why?

Can you tell me about a teacher who has made a significant impact on you?

What has been your most challenging subject or project, and how did you handle it?

MOM

# School zone

What is your favorite subject at school and why?

Can you tell me about a teacher who has made a significant impact on you?

What has been your most challenging subject or project, and how did you handle it?

# School zone

Have you faced any peer pressure? How do you deal with it?

How do you handle conflicts or disagreements with friends at school?

What skills have you learned at school that you think will help you in the future?

# School zone

Have you faced any peer pressure? How do you deal with it?

How do you handle conflicts or disagreements with friends at school?

What skills have you learned at school that you think will help you in the future?

# School zone

What's the best group project you've ever worked on? What made it successful?

What has been the most fun school event you've participated in?

Have school activities helped you discover any new interests or hobbies?

# School zone

What's the best group project you've ever worked on? What made it successful?

What has been the most fun school event you've participated in?

Have school activities helped you discover any new interests or hobbies?

# Teacher Appreciation Notes

Once a semester or year, choose a teacher each to write a thank you note to. It could be current teachers or one from the past. In the journal, draft the note, discussing why you appreciate this teacher and what impact they've had.

If comfortable, send the finalized note to the teacher, or keep it in the journal as a testament to their influence.

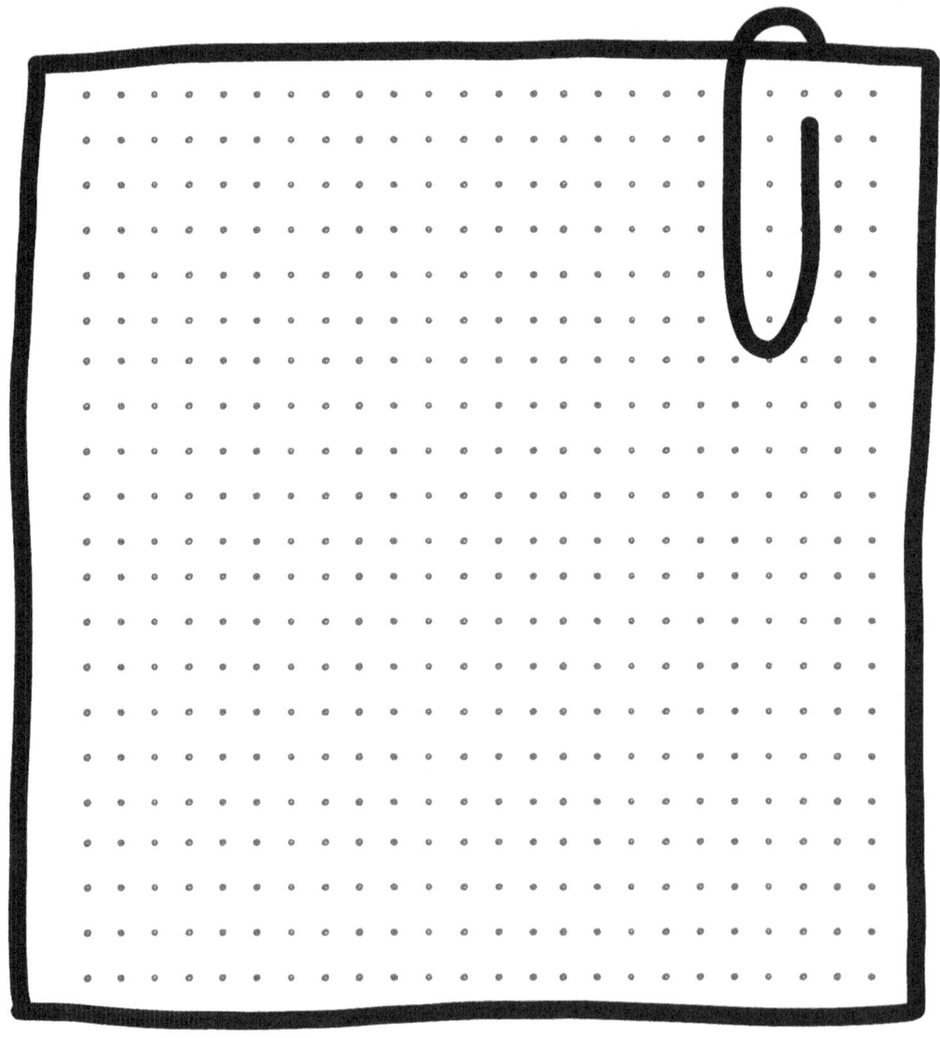

# Teacher Appreciation Notes

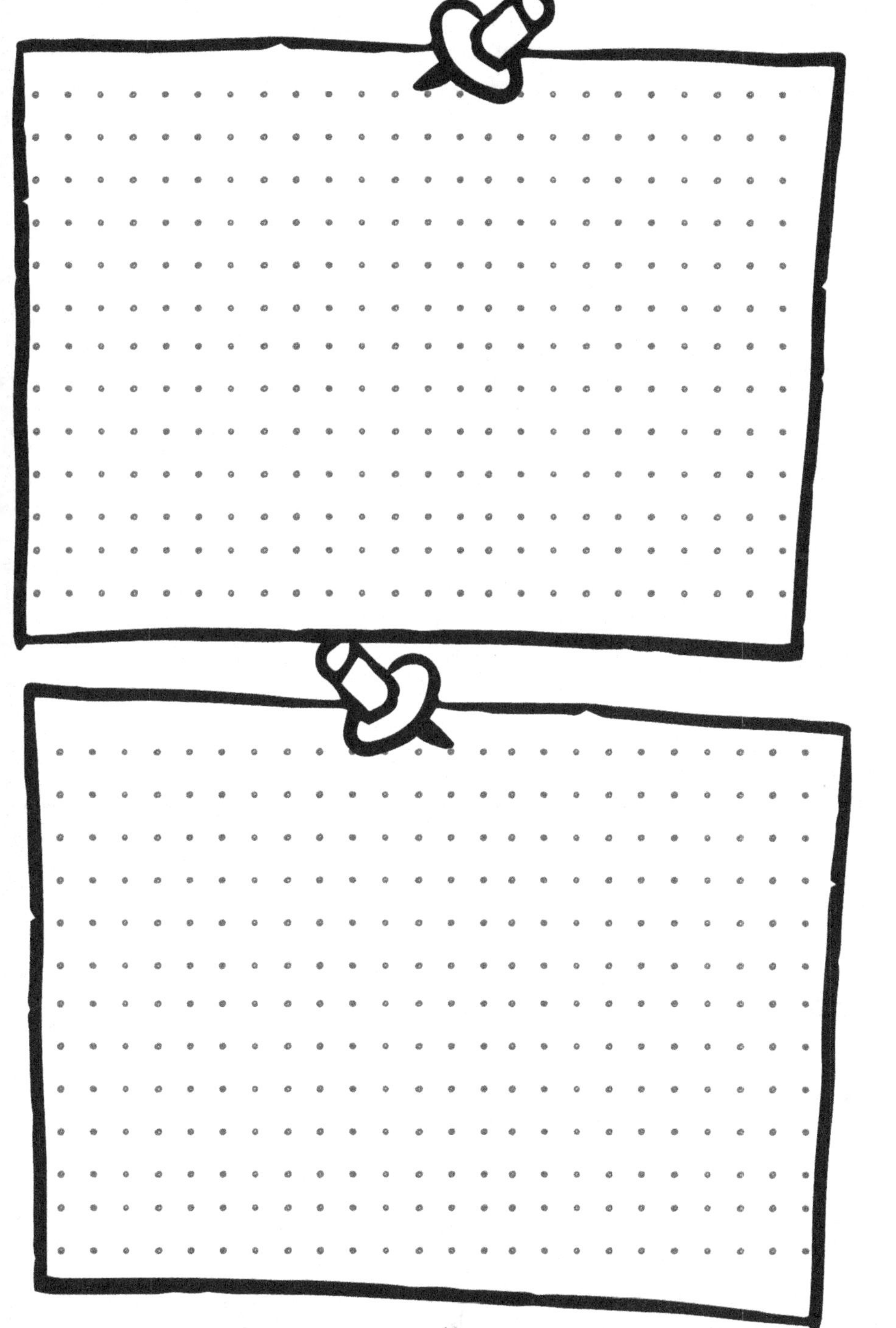

# Our Book/Movie Review Corner

Whenever you read a book or watch a movie together, write a short review. Rate it and mark whether you'd recommend it or not.

Title:.......................................................................................................

| | Did I enjoy it? | Do I recommend it? |
|---|---|---|
| Mom | ☆☆☆☆☆ | |
| Daughter | ☆☆☆☆☆ | |

Title:.......................................................................................................

| | Did I enjoy it? | Do I recommend it? |
|---|---|---|
| Mom | ☆☆☆☆☆ | |
| Daughter | ☆☆☆☆☆ | |

Title:.......................................................................................................

| | Did I enjoy it? | Do I recommend it? |
|---|---|---|
| Mom | ☆☆☆☆☆ | |
| Daughter | ☆☆☆☆☆ | |

Title:.......................................................................................................

| | Did I enjoy it? | Do I recommend it? |
|---|---|---|
| Mom | ☆☆☆☆☆ | |
| Daughter | ☆☆☆☆☆ | |

# Our Book/Movie Review Corner

Whenever you read a book or watch a movie together, write a short review. Rate it and mark whether you'd recommend it or not.

Title:.............................................................................................

| | Did I enjoy it? | Do I recommend it? |
|---|---|---|
| Mom | ☆☆☆☆☆ | |
| Daughter | ☆☆☆☆☆ | |

Title:.............................................................................................

| | Did I enjoy it? | Do I recommend it? |
|---|---|---|
| Mom | ☆☆☆☆☆ | |
| Daughter | ☆☆☆☆☆ | |

Title:.............................................................................................

| | Did I enjoy it? | Do I recommend it? |
|---|---|---|
| Mom | ☆☆☆☆☆ | |
| Daughter | ☆☆☆☆☆ | |

Title:.............................................................................................

| | Did I enjoy it? | Do I recommend it? |
|---|---|---|
| Mom | ☆☆☆☆☆ | |
| Daughter | ☆☆☆☆☆ | |

# Our Book/Movie Review Corner

Whenever you read a book or watch a movie together, write a short review. Rate it and mark whether you'd recommend it or not.

Title:........................................................................................................

| | Did I enjoy it? | Do I recommend it? |
|---|---|---|
| Mom | ☆☆☆☆☆ | |
| Daughter | ☆☆☆☆☆ | |

Title:........................................................................................................

| | Did I enjoy it? | Do I recommend it? |
|---|---|---|
| Mom | ☆☆☆☆☆ | |
| Daughter | ☆☆☆☆☆ | |

Title:........................................................................................................

| | Did I enjoy it? | Do I recommend it? |
|---|---|---|
| Mom | ☆☆☆☆☆ | |
| Daughter | ☆☆☆☆☆ | |

Title:........................................................................................................

| | Did I enjoy it? | Do I recommend it? |
|---|---|---|
| Mom | ☆☆☆☆☆ | |
| Daughter | ☆☆☆☆☆ | |

# Friendship and Relationships

# Friendship and Relationships

Who was your first friend, and what was the most memorable thing you did together?

What qualities do you value most in a friend?

Have you ever had a friendship end? What did that experience teach you about relationships?

# Friendship and Relationships

Who was your first friend, and what was the most memorable thing you did together?

What qualities do you value most in a friend?

Have you ever had a friendship end? What did that experience teach you about relationships?

# Friendship and Relationships

Who is your closest friend currently, and why do you think your bond is so strong?

Is there anything you feel you can't discuss with your friends but wish you could? Why?

How do you handle disagreements or conflicts in friendships? Can you share an example?

MOM

# Friendship and Relationships

Who is your closest friend currently, and why do you think your bond is so strong?

Is there anything you feel you can't discuss with your friends but wish you could? Why?

How do you handle disagreements or conflicts in friendships? Can you share an example?

# Friendship and Relationships

What role do you think trust plays in a relationship?

How do you know when someone is a true friend?

How do you think the way we communicate with friends has changed with technology?

MOM

# Friendship and Relationships

What role do you think trust plays in a relationship?

How do you know when someone is a true friend?

How do you think the way we communicate with friends has changed with technology?

# Starry Sky

Each star represents a friend or important person in your life. Write their names and then connect the stars with lines to create constellations that tell stories about your relationships.

# Starry Sky

Each star represents a friend or important person in your life. Connect stars with lines to form constellations that tell stories about your relationships.

# Comic Strip Confessions

Use comics to depict a humorous misunderstanding or a memorable moment from a friendship. Use dialogue bubbles to capture what was actually said versus what was understood.

Share and laugh about how these moments unfolded and how they were resolved.

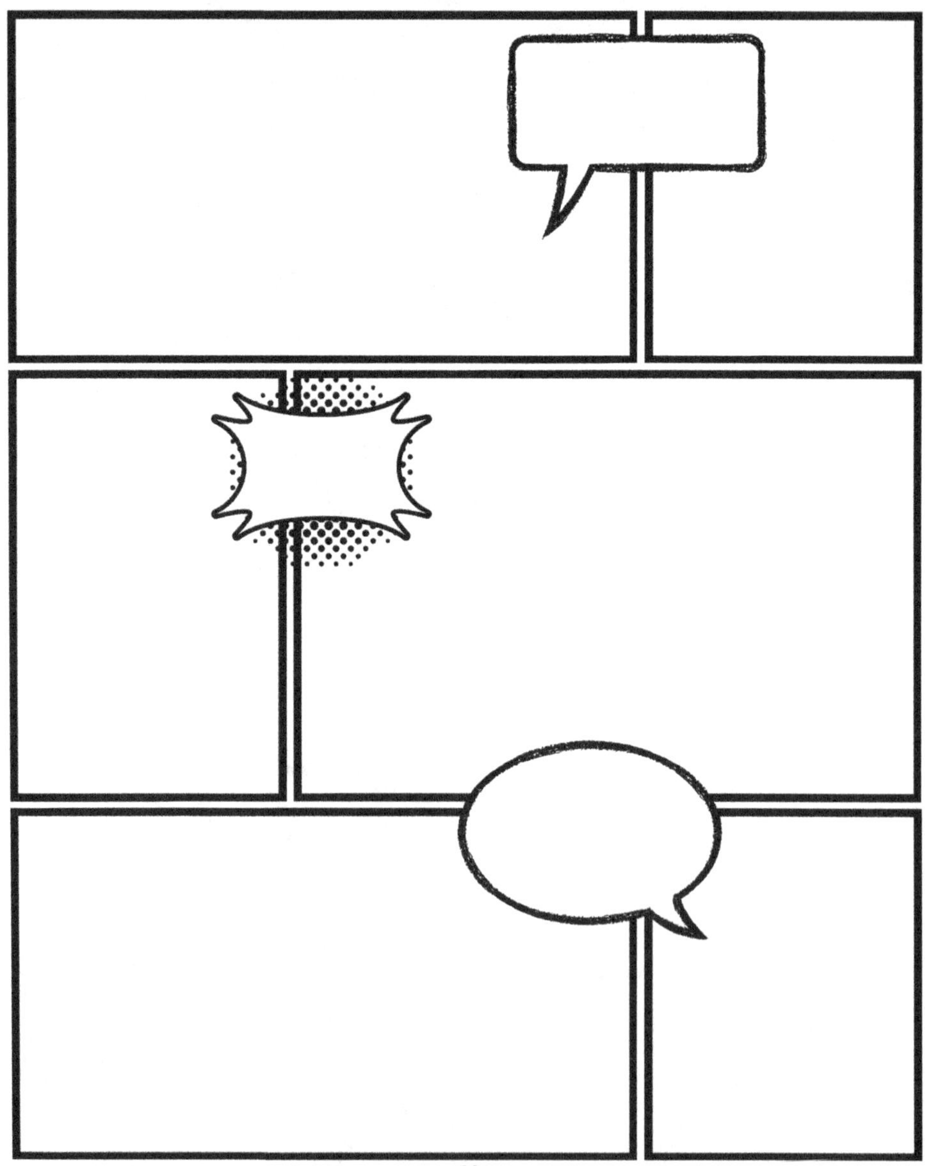

# Women's Wisdom

# Deep Conversations

This chapter definitely is the most personal and sensitive chapter of your shared journal. In this space you will discuss topics that often go unspoken.

Some of the questions will be based on mom's experience and some on daughter's curiosity, so the concept of this chapter is different.

Below you will find a list of topics related to growing up, first loves, experiences with the body and sexuality, as well as issues of self-acceptance, risks and life choices. They are only a spark for conversation. Decide for yourself which topics you want to cover, and if you want to jot down your thoughts and tips use the notebook provided in this section. If not, let these intimate conversations remain solely in your memory.

## Menstruation

- When did you get your first period, and what was it like for you?
- How did you learn about menstruation, and who taught you?
- Is there anything about menstruation that you wish you had known earlier?
- Are there any myths or misconceptions about menstruation that you've encountered?

## First Love

- Can you tell me about your first crush or love? What was it like?
- How did you handle heartbreak or rejection for the first time?
- How did you know you were ready to start dating?
- What advice would you give to someone experiencing their first love?

# Deep Conversations

## Sex and Intimacy

- How did you decide you were ready to become sexually active?
- What should I consider before deciding to have sex?
- Can we talk about consent? What does it mean, and why is it important?
- How important is it to maintain one's boundaries in intimate situations, and how can this be done?
- What are the most important things to know about safe sex?

## Self-Image

- How did you feel about your body image when you were my age?
- What advice can you give me about loving and accepting my body?
- What do you love most about how you look, and what would you change if you could?
- How do you deal with media portrayals of 'ideal' beauty standards?
- What can we do to help each other feel more confident about our bodies?

## Peer Pressure

- Can you recall a time when you gave in to peer pressure? What happened, and what did you learn from it?
- How do you differentiate between good and bad influences from friends?
- Have you ever helped a friend deal with peer pressure? What did you do?

## Addictions

- Have you ever felt pressured by friends or others at school to try drugs or alcohol?
- What would you do if someone offered you drugs or alcohol?
- What is the best way for someone to support their friends if they are struggling with issues like drinking or drug use?

# Deep Conversations

# Deep Conversations

# Deep Conversations

# Deep Conversations

# Compliments board

This activity is designed to build self-esteem and nurture a positive self-image for both of you through the exchange of heartfelt compliments.

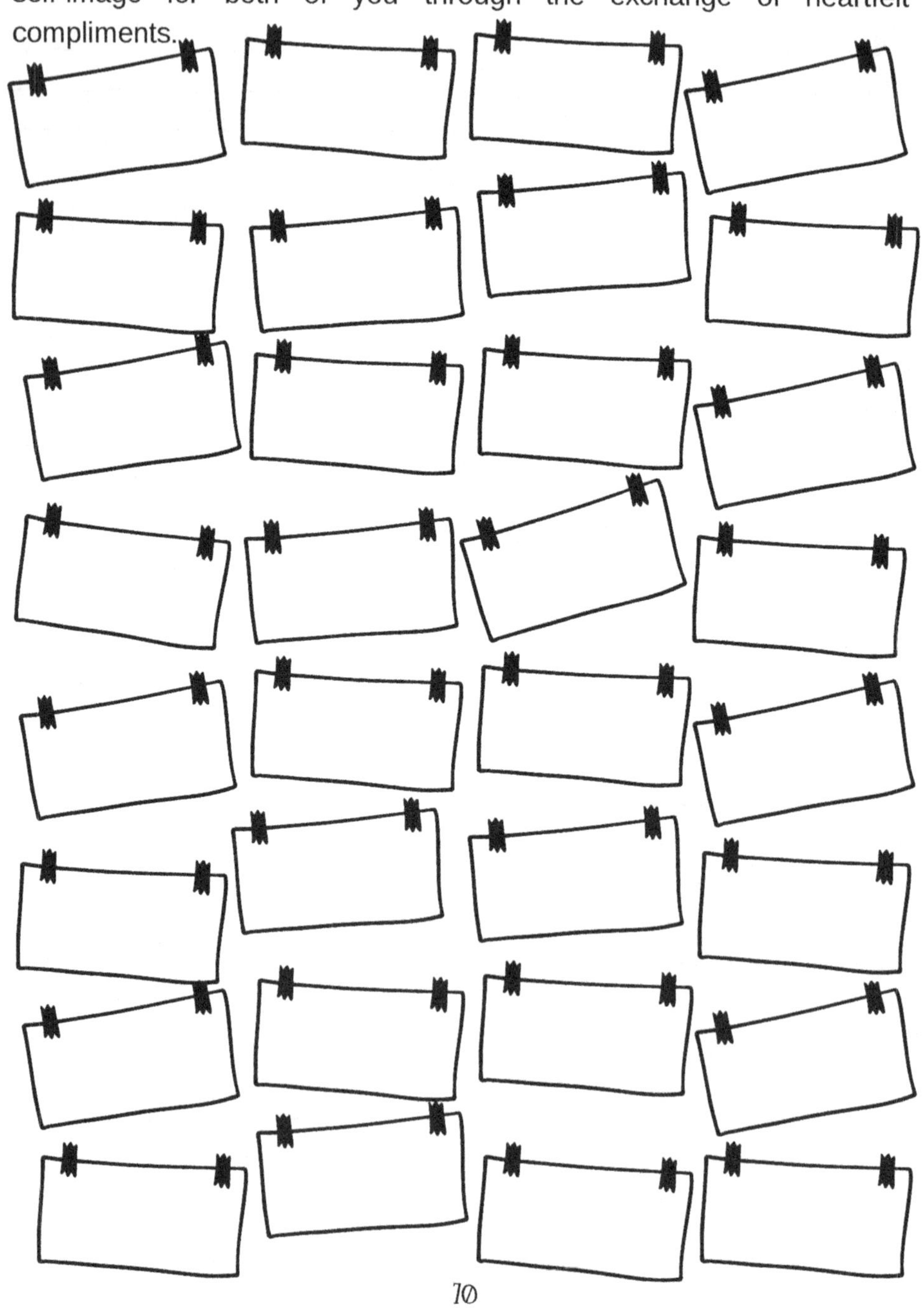

# Dreams and Desires

# What would you pack for your dream trip?

Your dream trip is coming up - Mother and Daughter.
What will you pack in your suitcase?
What do you not leave home without?
Write or draw what you are taking with you.

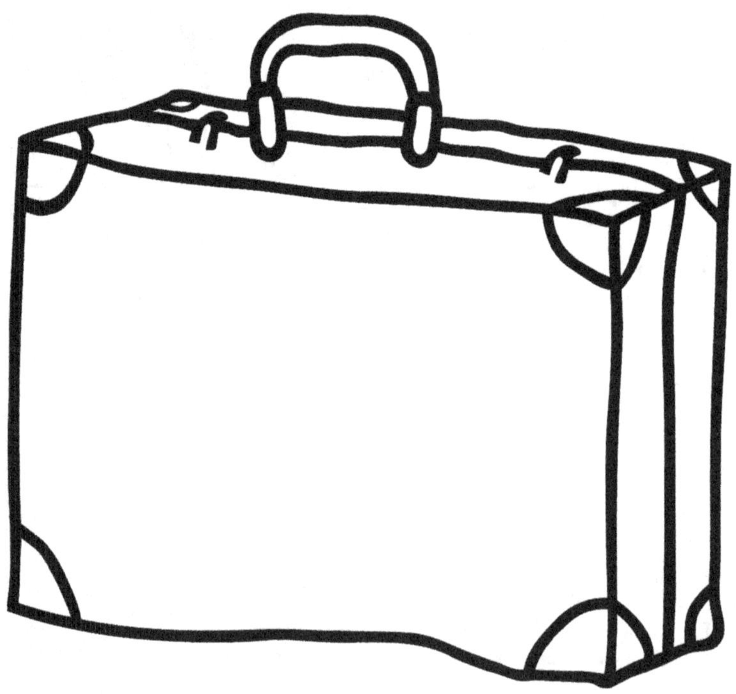

## What not to take so as not to spoil the fun?

# Dream tree

This is your Dream Tree, draw leaves or fruits
with your dreams written on them.
When you have finished, talk about them and how
you can support each other in achieving them.

# Dreams and Desires

If you could achieve one big dream in the next year, what would it be?

What kind of person do you hope to become?

MOM

# Dreams and Desires

If you could achieve one big dream in the next year, what would it be?

What kind of person do you hope to become?

# Dreams and Desires

What is something you've always wanted to learn or do, and what's stopping you?

What does your perfect day look like?

# Dreams and Desires

What is something you've always wanted to learn or do, and what's stopping you?

What does your perfect day look like?

# Dreams and Desires

Describe a desire you had as a child. Has it changed as you've grown?

Is there a dream or goal that scares you? What makes it intimidating?

MOM

# Dreams and Desires

Describe a desire you had as a child. Has it changed as you've grown?

Is there a dream or goal that scares you? What makes it intimidating?

# Mom's Vision Board Collage

Cut out the images and words that resonate with your dreams and arrange them on the page in a collage format. Use markers, stickers, or doodles to add extra flair.

# Daughter's Vision Board Collage

Cut out the images and words that resonate with your dreams and arrange them on the page in a collage format. Use markers, stickers, or doodles to add extra flair.

# If I Could Change the World...

Reflect on what you would change about the world if you had the power. Write down your ideas and why these changes are important to you. Discuss how you can start making small changes today that align with these big dreams.

# Gratitude and Appreciations

# Gratitude Journal

In this mini 'Gratitude Journal', write down something you are grateful to each other for. It could be a character trait, a gesture, time spent together or help in a difficult situation. This practice strengthens positive relationships and teaches you to appreciate the little things.

Mom | Daughter

Day 1

Day 2

Day 3

# Gratitude Journal

## Day 4

## Day 5

## Day 6

## Day 7

# Gratitude and Appreciations

What's something I did for you recently that you're thankful for, and why?

Is there a particular challenge or low point in our lives for which you now feel grateful? Why?

What's something about the world around you that you're thankful for today?

# Gratitude and Appreciations

What's something I did for you recently that you're thankful for, and why?

Is there a particular challenge or low point in our lives for which you now feel grateful? Why?

What's something about the world around you that you're thankful for today?

# Gratitude Jar

This jar is for drawing or listing items that represent things you're grateful for.

# Adventures and Experiences

# Adventures and Experiences

What has been our most memorable adventure together? What made it so special?

What is the funniest or most unexpected thing that happened to us on a vacation?

Of all the places we have visited, which would you love to return to, and why?

# Adventures and Experiences

What has been our most memorable adventure together? What made it so special?

What is the funniest or most unexpected thing that happened to us on a vacation?

Of all the places we have visited, which would you love to return to, and why?

# Adventures and Experiences

If we could go anywhere in the world together, where would it be and why?

What is one adventure activity you've always wanted to try but haven't yet?

How have our adventures together changed the way you view the world?

MOM

# Adventures and Experiences

If we could go anywhere in the world together, where would it be and why?

What is one adventure activity you've always wanted to try but haven't yet?

How have our adventures together changed the way you view the world?

# Adventures and Experiences

What's the most unusual food you've tried during your travels? Did you like it?

If you could go on a road trip with any three people (famous, friends, or fictional), who would they be and why?

If you could invent a new sport or game for us to play on our next vacation, what would it be and what are the rules?

MOM

# Adventures and Experiences

What's the most unusual food you've tried during your travels? Did you like it?

If you could go on a road trip with any three people (famous, friends, or fictional), who would they be and why?

If you could invent a new sport or game for us to play on our next vacation, what would it be and what are the rules?

# Adventure Map

Use markers or pins to denote places you have visited together. Add dates and short notes or anecdotes about each adventure, capturing memorable moments or feelings from the trip. Use a different color or style of marker to indicate places you both dream of visiting.

# Local Exploration Challenge

Make a list of local places you both have never visited but are interested in exploring. Challenge yourselves to visit one new place each month and document the experience with photos and journal entries. After each visit, write about your impressions, the best moments, and anything surprising you learned.

1. ..........................................................................................
2. ..........................................................................................
3. ..........................................................................................
4. ..........................................................................................
5. ..........................................................................................
6. ..........................................................................................
7. ..........................................................................................
8. ..........................................................................................
9. ..........................................................................................
10. ..........................................................................................
11. ..........................................................................................
12. ..........................................................................................
13. ..........................................................................................
14. ..........................................................................................
15. ..........................................................................................

# Local Exploration Challenge

# Local Exploration Challenge

# Hopes for the Future

# Hopes for the Future

As you think about the future, what's one dream that excites you the most?

What's one skill you'd like to learn that you think will help you in the future?

As you grow older, what's one thing you hope will never change about our relationship?

MOM

# Hopes for the Future

As you think about the future, what's one dream that excites you the most?

What's one skill you'd like to learn that you think will help you in the future?

As you grow older, what's one thing you hope will never change about our relationship?

# Hopes for the Future

Where in the world would you most like to live, and why?

What do you hope the world will be like in 20 years?

# Hopes for the Future

Where in the world would you most like to live, and why?

What do you hope the world will be like in 20 years?

# A letter to My Daughter

Write letters to each other. Share what you value in each other, your hopes for the future and your wishes for the other person.

# A letter to My Mom

# Goal Setting Workshop

Together, create a list of short-term and long-term goals. Discuss why these goals are important and what achieving them would mean.

| Short-term | long-term |
|---|---|

# Notes

# Notes

# Notes

# Notes

# Notes

Made in the USA
Las Vegas, NV
03 May 2025

21654163R00066